# Miniature Quilling

## DIANE BODEN CRANE

SEARCH PRESS

First published in Great Britain 2007

Search Press Limited
Wellwood, North Farm Road,
Tunbridge Wells, Kent TN2 3DR

Text copyright © Diane Boden Crane 2007

Photographs by Steve Crispe, Search Press Studios; and
Roddy Paine Photographic Studio

Photographs and design copyright © Search Press Ltd. 2007

ISBN 10: 1-84448-205-7
ISBN 13: 978-1-84448-205-4

The Publishers and author can accept no responsibility for
any consequences arising from the information, advice or
instructions given in this publication.

Readers are permitted to reproduce any of the items in this
book for their personal use, or for the purposes of selling
for charity, free of charge and without the prior permission
of the Publishers. Any use of the items for commercial
purposes is not permitted without the prior permission of
the Publishers.

Suppliers
If you have difficulty in obtaining any of the materials and
equipment mentioned in this book, then please visit the
Search Press website for details of suppliers:
www.searchpress.com

Publisher's note

All the step-by-step photographs in this book feature
the author, Diane Boden Crane, demonstrating miniature
quilling. No models have been used.

Conversion table

All of the measurements in this book are given in both
metric (millimetres) and imperial (inches) units. The
widths of the paper strips used, in metric units, are
3mm, 2mm, 1mm, 1.5mm and 0.5mm. Their approximate
imperial equivalents are as follows:

| | | | |
|---|---|---|---|
| 3mm | $1/8$in | 1.5mm | $1/16$in |
| 2mm | $1/12$in | 0.5mm | $1/48$in |
| 1mm | $1/24$in | | |

Dedication
I would like to dedicate this book to my dear husband, Tris.
Thank you for all your loving support and encouragement
in giving me the time and space to complete the projects,
without complaint – especially in our first few months
of marriage! This book is my gift to you – especially the
chocolates – I know they are your favourite. I love you
'quillions', your E.L.W.M.D.

Acknowledgements
My thanks to the team at Search Press for their
combined skills, especially Katie, my editor, for
her friendly efficiency and attention to detail.
Photographing the quilling for this book was
no easy task, so my grateful thanks are due
to Steve and Roddy for their great patience in
photographing such tiny pieces of paper and
keeping their sense of humour! Not for the
first time, I would like to pay tribute to the
enthusiasm and good humour of 'my quilling
ladies'. The projects in this book would not have
come to fruition but for my need to produce
original designs for them. Thank you all for your
continued support and friendship, which means a
great deal.

'That everyone may eat and drink, and find
satisfaction in all his toil – this is the gift of God.'
Ecclesiastes 3 v.13

'Whatever your hand finds to do, do it with all
your might...'
Ecclesiastes 9 v.10

# Contents

# Introduction

One of the things I like most about the craft of quilling is that it can be practised using a range of paper widths, depending on the effect you want to achieve. Although I first learnt the craft using paper strips 3mm wide (there was very little 2mm paper available at the time), I soon had the desire to create more delicate designs using finer strips. One answer was to cut 3mm strips in half down the centre, but as time went on, 2mm strips became much more readily available. Today, we are spoilt for choice when it comes to the colour and finish of narrow strips. No longer is 2mm-wide paper the Cinderella of the quilling world!

*These quilled chocolates look good enough to eat (see page 30).*

*Stationery and an aperture frame decorated with quilled autumn leaves (see page 23).*

Through the pages of this book, I hope to inspire readers with designs that concentrate on fine quilling. Some parts still call for 3mm-wide paper of course, but 2mm, 1mm, 1.5mm and occasionally 0.5mm-wide strips have also been used. The technique of spiralling features quite heavily in some of the projects. It is an ideal use of very narrow paper and adds a different texture and dimension that contrasts well with more traditional quilled shapes. However, many of the familiar basic shapes have still been used and there is much that will be familiar to the seasoned quiller.

I have tried to illustrate a number of applications for miniature quilling, from conventional greetings cards and photograph frames to napkin rings and a selection of quilled chocolates that look good enough to eat!

In my experience as a quilling teacher, students seldom look back once they have experienced the satisfaction of working with narrow paper strips. Even though the difference may be only a millimetre, the results appear much more delicate and pleasing to the eye. One phrase I have heard repeatedly over the years has been, 'I never knew quilling could be this small'! It is my hope that this book will give quillers the confidence to experiment with narrow strips to produce miniature quilling of which they can be proud.

# Materials and equipment

The chief requirements for miniature quilling are paper strips, a quilling tool, scissors and glue. You can add to these basic items as you go along.

## Paper strips

Quilling strips come in packs that have been pre-cut to size and can be bought in a variety of different widths. This book uses paper 2mm and 3mm wide, although sometimes these strips are cut down to 1mm wide (for example for spiralling), 1.5mm and occasionally 0.5mm wide (for example for decorating the chocolates). The papers are easier to work with if they are encouraged out of their figure of eight formation. This can be achieved by laying them flat in a shallow tray or box.

A standard British quilling strip is approximately 450mm (17¾in) in length. You should find that papers 2mm wide are readily available through quilling suppliers and it is possible to order paper that is 1mm wide. However, often it is more convenient and economical to simply cut the paper to the required width yourself. This may seem a daunting task at first, but like everything else, patience brings its own reward!

Occasionally, I have used pearlised and metallic strips that have a treated edge. This effect becomes more pronounced once the paper has been coiled or wound.

**Tip**
For each of the projects in this book, you will need the following basic items of equipment: quilling tool, scissors, PVA glue in a fine-tip applicator, cocktail sticks, metric ruler, metal ruler, scalpel, cutting mat and pencil.

# Equipment

Various **quilling tools** are available commercially, and the finer the tool the better, especially when it comes to miniature quilling. Try to find a tool that has a fine slit. **PVA glue** is the most widely used glue and is ideal for the job. Try to use very small amounts – you will find a **fine-tip applicator** an enormous help. It dispenses a tiny dot of glue and is controlled by a gentle squeeze of the bottle. **Cocktail sticks** are invaluable when picking up very small pieces of quilling. Alternatively, some people prefer using **fine tweezers**. A pair of good quality **scissors** is an essential part of your equipment. Make sure the blades have short, sharp points to give you an accurate cut. For making spirals, I generally use **rose wire**. This is a fine wire that needs to be handled with care as it bends easily. You will need an ordinary metric **ruler** for measuring the lengths of your strips, and a metal one for cutting card etc.

Other useful items include a **pair of compasses**, a **2H pencil** (this gives a good sharp line) and a **scalpel**. Cutting on a **self-healing mat** saves your blade and the surface of the dining room table! **Round-headed pins** in different sizes are ideal when making a dome out of a solid coil, and **chalk pastels** are great for backgrounds – they come in a wide range of colours and are very economical to use.

## Papers and cards

It is a good idea to collect a selection of papers, cards, etc. to set off your quilling. Several projects use a plain box as a base – you might be lucky and find the exact colour you want, or you may end up having to cover the box with paper. I found saved foil wrappers very useful when it came to the quilled chocolates (see pages 30–35)! For the project on page 24, I used a blank card frame, obtainable from good craft stores.

Tissue paper is a handy addition to the quiller's store, as it rolls up beautifully when making paper sticks.

# Basic techniques

If you look closely at a paper strip you will notice that the two sides are different. The 'right' side looks and feels smooth at the edges where the paper turns down very slightly. Consequently, the 'wrong' side of the paper appears rough at the edges. Try to get into the habit of always rolling the paper with the smooth side on the outside of your coil, as this will make your quilling look more even. Although this book is about miniature quilling, do not be tempted to roll the paper too tightly! The paper lengths may be quite short in some cases, but there still needs to be a certain amount of 'give' in the coil to enable you to make a well-defined shape.

If you are new to quilling, practise rolling with 3mm-wide strips to begin with, before attempting to quill with finer strips.

## A basic coil

The secret of good quilling is to keep an even tension as you roll the paper strip. This will produce a more regular, evenly spaced coil.

1 Line up the end of the paper strip on the quilling tool.

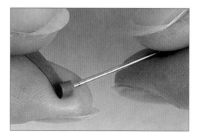

2 Turn the tool so that the paper winds tightly around it.

3 Release the coil.

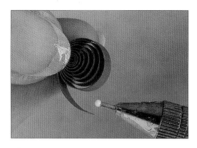

4 Put a dot of PVA glue on the end of the strip. Try to use as little glue as possible for a neat finish.

5 Seal the coil by pressing down firmly on the seam using a cocktail stick.

*A finished basic coil.*

# Basic shapes

All of the shapes shown below are used in the projects in this book. They are all made from a basic coil.

**Teardrop**
*Pinch the coil into a point using your thumb and forefinger.*

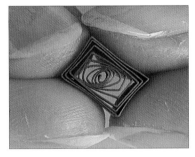

**Eye shape**
*Pinch the coil at both ends using using your thumbs and forefingers.*

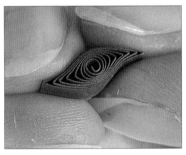

**Oval**
*Gently squeeze the coil between your thumb and forefinger, with the join on one side.*

**Square**
*Make an eye shape, then pinch the other two sides to form a square.*

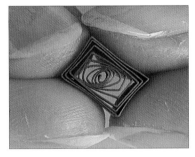

**Rectangle**
*Make in the same way as a square, but with two long sides and two short sides.*

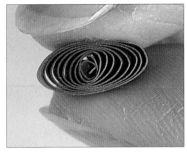

**Leaf shape**
*Make an eye shape, then gently press two opposite edges together.*

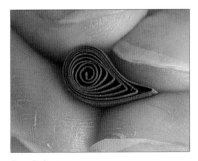

**Petal shape**
*Pinch the coil into a teardrop, pulling the point over to one side.*

**Heart shape**
*Make a teardrop, then put a dent in the rounded end using your thumb nail. Alternatively, use the point of a cocktail stick.*

---

**Tip**
When making shapes, always pinch your coil at the glued join to help hide it.

9

# Peg

As the peg is made of solid paper, it is worth taking the trouble to smooth out the layers and tidy the centre, which will improve its appearance.

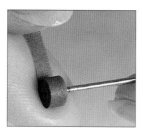

1 Roll a tight coil, but don't let it go.

2 Glue the end of the paper strip, keeping the coil tight, while it is still on the tool. Remove the tool and tap the peg down to even out the layers.

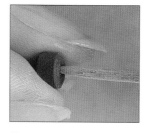

3 Place a cocktail stick in the centre of the peg and twist it to make the centre smooth.

*A finished peg.*

# A solid coil

This is not an easy technique to master but is well worth the effort. The coil is formed using the fingers only, without the use of a quilling tool, to avoid forming a hole in the centre. Try to keep the coil very tight as you roll, and don't let go too soon!

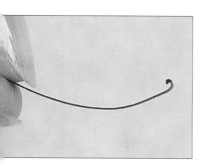

1 Turn over the end of the paper strip as tightly as possible.

2 Roll the strip by hand into a tight coil.

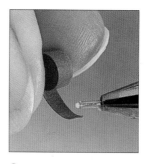

3 Apply a dot of PVA glue to the end of the strip, keeping the coil tight.

*A finished solid coil.*

# Spiral

Spiralling takes practice to achieve a uniform result. As with rolling coils, the secret is in maintaining the tension – holding the paper taut while rotating the wire. Spirals work well using 1mm- or 1.5mm-wide strips.

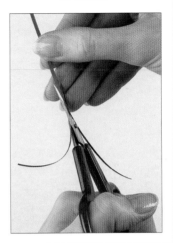

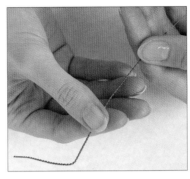

1 Dampen the end of a 1mm paper strip and wind it on to a piece of thin wire at a 45° angle. Hold the paper and twist the wire, not the other way round.

2 When you have wound on the whole strip, carefully remove the wire by pushing the paper off the end.

3 Tighten up the spiral by pulling and twisting it at the same time.

# Paper sticks

The important things to remember when rolling paper sticks are to roll around the wire as closely as possible and to roll centrally, keeping the ends even.

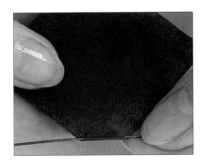

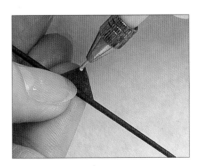

1 Fold the corner of a small sheet of tissue paper over a length of thin wire and glue it down using PVA.

2 Roll the tissue paper tightly around the wire.

3 Glue the end of the paper in place and remove the wire.

# Daisies and Lavender

This simple floral design is used here to create a greetings card. It combines two different ways of using an aperture. A thick card template is used to make a sturdy paper frame to support the lavender, and the daisies are attached to a lattice background, which has been created with double-thickness paper strips.

The open space behind the quilling really shows off the beauty of the craft, which can sometimes be lost when the quilling is simply glued to a solid background. Care must be taken to ensure that the quilling touches the inside of the frame at various points so that it is well supported.

## You will need

*Lavender sprigs, 3mm strips*
36 mauve strips, 45mm
(1¾in) long

1 pale green strip, 450mm
(18in) long

4 pale green strips, 225mm
(9in) long

*Daisies, 2mm strips*
42 white strips, 75mm
(3in) long

6 yellow strips, 75mm
(3in) long

12 mid-green strips, 56mm
(2¼in) long

*Raised frames, 3mm strips*
3 mid-green strips, 450mm
(18in) long

*Lattice windows, 2mm strips*
7 pale green strips, 450mm
(18in) long

2 mid-green strips, 450mm
(18in) long

*Other materials*
5 small pieces of cardboard,
44 x 25mm (1¾ x 1in), for
frame template

White card, 210 x 150mm
(8¾ x 6in), scored in half
to make a card blank 210 x
75mm (8¾ x 3in)

Mauve card, 205 x 70mm (8
x 2¾in)

Pale green paper, 205 x
145mm (8 x 5¾in),
for insert

1 Photocopy the template below at 200 per cent, and copy it on to mauve card. Glue the mauve card on to one side of the white card using PVA glue. Working on a cutting mat, cut out the apertures using a craft knife and metal ruler.

2 For the lattice windows, glue two 2mm pale green strips together using PVA glue. Work on one 50mm (2in) section at a time.

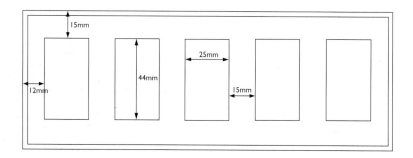

*Template for the card,
half actual size.*

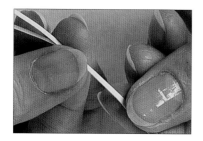

3 Stick the two strips together by holding them at the sides between your thumb and forefinger, and pulling the paper through. Do this for each of the seven pale green strips, cutting the seventh strip in half and gluing the two halves together.

*Template for the grid, used to align the paper strips in step 4 below. Reproduced actual size.*

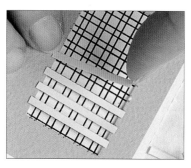

4 Cut the double-thickness strips into eight 28mm (1¼in) strips and five 47mm (1¾in) strips for each lattice window. Place the grid behind the aperture and use it to position the horizontal strips accurately. Glue them in place using a small dab of PVA glue applied to the card at each end.

5 Attach the vertical strips in the same way, applying glue to the card at each end and to the horizontals to secure them.

6 Frame each lattice window using the 2mm mid-green strips. Glue on the verticals first, then the horizontals. Apply the glue to the card, lay on the green strip then cut the strip to the correct length.

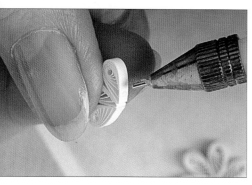

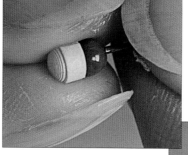

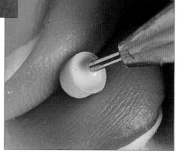

7 For each daisy, make seven white teardrops and glue them together in a circle.

8 For the centre of each daisy, make a yellow peg and dome it by pushing up the centre using the round end of a pin. Seal the inside with PVA glue.

9 Glue a yellow peg to the centre of each daisy, then attach two daisies to each lattice. Apply the glue to the back of the daisies, not to the lattice. Make four mid-green eye shapes for the leaves and attach two to each daisy using the end of a cocktail stick.

10 Build the raised frames for the remaining two windows around a 3mm (¼in) thick block, the same size as the apertures, made by gluing together layers of cardboard.

11 Wrap a 3mm mid-green strip around the block four times. Apply glue in between each layer. Attach a 450mm (18in) strip first, then continue with a second strip to complete the frame. Cut off the end of the second strip.

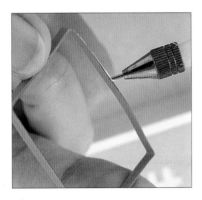

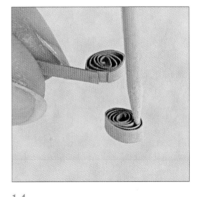

12 Remove the frame from the block, and apply glue along the lower edge.

13 Attach the frame to the card.

14 For the lavender stems, cut the 450mm (18in) pale green strip into two equal lengths and glue them together to make a double-thickness strip (see step 3). For each sprig, cut a 45mm (1¾in) long stem from the double-thickness strip and make nine mauve ovals for the flowers. Attach two flowers at the top of the stem.

15 Work down the stem in pairs, always applying the glue to the stem and not to the flowers.

16 Complete the sprig by gluing the ninth flower between the pair at the top.

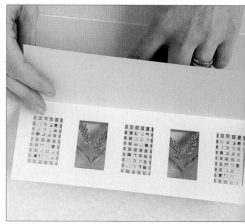

17 Fit one lavender in the frame, gluing it at the points where it touches the frame. Fit in the second, smaller, sprig, trimming the stem to size.

18 Finally, make four pale green leaf shapes and attach one leaf shape to each lavender sprig, postioning the leaves using a cocktail stick.

19 Fold the pale green paper in half to form an insert, and glue it in place along the top inner edge of the card.

*The completed card.*

The frame and lattice techniques described in the project can be used on their own to good effect. The greetings card uses pegs in between the frames to support the design. Both the box and the card feature a single lavender stem, suspended by a thin spiral of paper. The basic technique has been adapted further to create place settings.

# Autumn Leaves

Every autumn I marvel at the variety of colours and shapes of the falling leaves. This design uses just a few leaf patterns, but these can be created in a number of autumnal colours to make an interesting design.

   The leaves would look good glued to a plain wooden box, or alternatively you could use a card box that has been covered in brown parcel paper first, similar to the one shown here. The acorn and oak leaf gift tag continues the theme.

   This design is worked entirely in 2mm-wide paper strips in a range of browns, reds and yellows.

## Oak leaf

1 Make six small petal shapes, and glue two together at the pointed end so they curve outwards. Make a small teardrop and glue it between them to form the top of the leaf.

2 Attach two more pairs of petal shapes. For the base, make an oval, then put a dent in one side and wrap it round the end of the leaf.

*The completed oak leaf.*

# Sycamore, horse chestnut and maple leaves

*The range of leaves I have created in this group are shown opposite. They consist of seven or five eye or leaf shapes arranged in a circle, with a stem made from a short, double thickness paper strip at the base. The shapes can either all be the same size, or vary, with the largest at the top of the leaf, and the smallest at its base. The instructions below are for the larger leaf shown top left, but can easily be adapted to suit which ever leaf type you choose to make.*

1 Glue three large eye shapes together to form the top of the leaf, then glue two medium-sized eye shapes below these.

2 Attach the two small eye shapes at the bottom to complete the leaf.

3 Apply glue to the inside edges of the lower two leaves and insert the stem.

# Ivy leaf

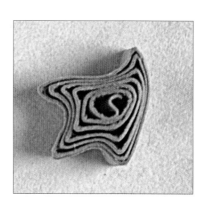

1 Start with an oval, and pinch the top to make three points.

2 Pinch the other end in the same way to form a total of five points.

3 Alternatively, form the other end into a single, curved point, as you would for a petal shape.

# Ash, elder and rowan leaves

These leaves, shown opposite, consist of two or three pairs of eye or leaf shapes arranged down a stem, with a single shape at the top. As before, the stems are made from a short, double-thickness strip. The instructions below are for a larger leaf, like the one shown top left, but can easily be adapted to suit which ever leaf type you choose to make.

Apply glue to the stem, and position the shapes using a cocktail stick. Allow each shape or pair of shapes to dry before moving on to the next.

# Decorating the box

Make a selection of leaf shapes in a variety of sizes and colours, and arrange them in an S-shaped pattern on the box lid. Make some single leaf and eye shapes as well to fill in any gaps in your design. Position the shapes first, then glue them all down when you are happy with your arrangement.

# The tag

1 For each of the five leaves, start with an oval and pinch it at both ends to form six points.

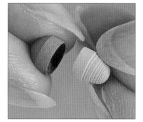

2 Make the acorns from two solid, domed coils. Make the cup slightly wider using a longer paper strip so that the nut fits inside it comfortably. Glue the nut inside the cup.

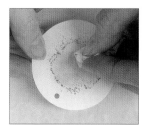

3 Colour the centre of the tag using pale brown chalk pastel applied with a piece of crumpled soft tissue paper.

4 Make two stems, 25mm (1in) long, from double thickness strips and glue them to the card along their thin edge.

5 Glue on the acorns and leaves. Complete the tag by threading a spiral made from a 1mm red paper strip (cut from a 2mm strip; see page 11) through the hole.

*The completed box and tag.*

The leaf sections on the napkin rings have been edged individually with gold- or copper-edged quilling strips. The leaves have been made following the same methods as in the project, before being arranged and glued to the rings.

The napkin rings have been made from sections of card tube – the type found in the centre of a kitchen roll. They have been covered with a decorative paper and trimmed with paper strips in brown and gold.

In the picture below, a selection of different-coloured leaves have been used to decorate stationery. The leaves on the greetings card have been carefully arranged around the aperture before being glued down. The background has been first coloured using chalk pastels (see page 24). This card could also be used as a photograph frame.

# Butterflies

The subject of butterflies continues to be a popular choice for those who enjoy quilling. Their wings can be made in a number of different ways, but I have chosen to quill them using conventional shapes with a 'paper bead' for the body section.

Limiting the number of colours used brings simplicity to the design and it is interesting to note how the colours appear different depending on the order in which they are used. Originally, the butterflies were flying around on the photograph frame, but they looked a little lost. I later decided to add leaves and stems to the background, which gave them something to 'sit' on and drew the design together. Sometimes, leaving a design for a while and coming back to it at a later stage allows you to view it differently and so make improvements to it.

You will need to make seven butterflies all together for this project; make each one using different-coloured paper strips for the wings.

1 Sprinkle the larger sheet of pale green paper with shavings from a yellow chalk pastel. Blend in the colour using a piece of crumpled soft tissue paper, then apply green chalk pastel.

2 Blend in the green pastel.

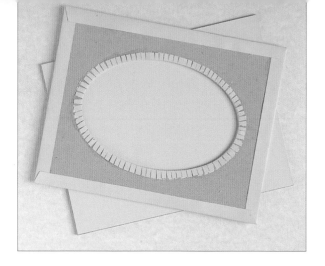

3  Use the coloured paper to cover the front of the frame. Cut off the corners of the paper and fold the edges of the paper behind the frame. Glue them in place. Cut out the aperture, leaving a 10mm (½in) border. Snip into the border, fold it behind the aperture and glue it in place. Cover the back of the frame using the other sheet of pale green paper.

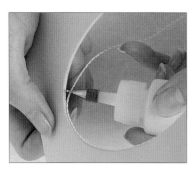

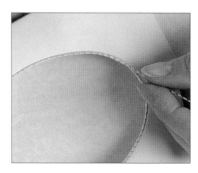

4  Make a spiral from a 1.5mm yellow strip. Apply glue to the lower edge of the inside of the frame and attach the spiral. Work in 50mm (2in) sections.

5  Make a spiral from a 1.5mm green strip, and attach this to the inside of the frame above the yellow spiral. Apply glue to both the yellow spiral and the edge of the frame to secure it.

6  Make a full length green spiral, and attach it to the frame to form the main stems. Start at the top of the frame on the left, then take the spiral round the base of the aperture and up the right-hand side. The right- and left-hand sides should be mirror images of each other. Apply the glue to the frame, not to the spiral, and work in 50mm (2in) sections.

7  Make the other stems and attach them in the same way, cutting the spirals to the correct length after they have been glued to the frame.

The completed stems.

8  Make twelve leaf shapes and attach them to the frame. Apply the glue to the backs of leaves and position them using a cocktail stick.

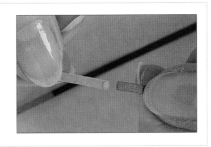

**Tip**

For the butterfly wings you need to glue two different-coloured strips together. Apply a dab of glue to the end of one strip and stick the other strip over the top of it.

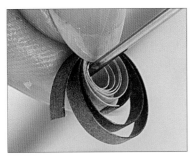

9 For the upper wings, glue together a purple and a mauve strip, and roll up the strip into a coil. Unwind the coil until the centre is large enough to hold a peg.

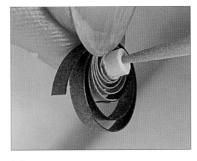

10 Place a pale yellow peg made from the 45mm-long paper strip in the centre of the coil using a cocktail stick.

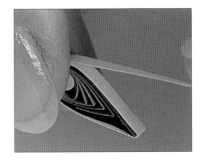

11 Make the coil into a teardrop, and wrap the 112mm pale yellow strip around the outside. Join it on at the tip of the teardrop, wrap it around three times, glue down the end and cut off the excess.

12 For the lower wings, make a mauve teardrop, then wrap around it three times with a purple strip, then again with a yellow strip. Make two pairs of wings, each consisting of an upper and a lower wing glued together at their tips. Glue the two pairs of wings together.

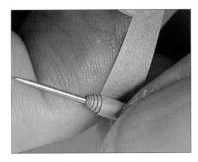

13 For the butterflies' bodies, coil the triangular piece of brown parcel paper around a long pin, starting at the base of the triangle. Glue down the end and remove the pin.

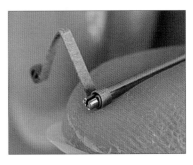

14 For the antennae, fold the 30mm (1¼in) length of 1mm brown paper strip in half and make a coil at each end. Seal each coil with glue.

15 Glue the antennae into the end of the body, and glue the body to the wings, applying the glue to the wings and then laying the body on top.

16 Make seven butterflies using different-coloured strips and glue them to the frame.

*The completed frame.*

The delicate nature of butterflies lends itself perfectly to glassware. The butterflies and leaves on the glass vase shown on the left have been made using pearlised paper, which gives them a beautiful sheen. They have been attached to the vase using small squares of double-sided sticky tape.

Spiralling comes into its own in the greetings card shown below. A length of spiral has been threaded through a series of pegs to create an open framework on which to rest the butterflies. For the smaller butterflies, simply halve the measurements.

At the other end of the scale, the box shown below has been decorated with butterflies twice the size of those made in the project. Spiralling has been used to complete the design.

# Chocolates

This project is great fun to work on as it provides a good deal of scope to use your imagination once the basic chocolate shapes have been mastered. I have found it very useful to keep the identification charts from boxes of chocolates to provide further inspiration. Not every subject translates well into quilling, but these chocolates work wonderfully well, and really do look 'edible'! I have seen many people do a double take when looking at them for the first time.

The colour of the paper strips is an important factor, so try to use strips that resemble chocolate as closely as possible. As purple is such a popular choice for chocolate packaging, I have chosen to use it as the base for the chocolate box, and in different shades for the variations.

## Basic chocolate shapes

### Diamond
Make two squares, pinch each of them into a diamond shape and glue one on top of the other.

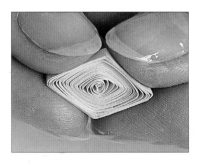

### Oval
Make two ovals, dome the centre of one of them and seal it with glue, then glue the two ovals together.

## You will need

**Basic chocolate shapes**

*Diamond, 3mm strips*
2 strips, 675mm (27in) long, made from a 450mm (18in) strip joined to a 225mm (9in) strip

*Oval, 3mm strips*
2 strips, 675mm (27in) long, made from a 450mm (18in) strip joined to a 225mm (9in) strip

*Dome, 3mm strips*
1 strip, 1125mm (45in) long, made from 2 x 450mm (18in) strips and a 225mm (9in) strip joined together

*Rectangle, 3mm strips*
5 strips, 225mm (9in) long

*Circle, 3mm strips*
2 strips, 1125mm (45in) long, made from 2 x 450mm (18in) strips and a 225mm (9in) strip joined together

**Decorations**
Various 1mm and 0.5mm paper strips
Small piece of purple foil

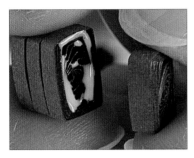

**Rectangle**
Make five small rectangles and glue them together, one on top of the other, to form a block.

**Circle**
Make two solid coils and slightly dome one of them. Glue the two coils together.

**Dome**
Make a solid coil and dome the centre. Apply glue inside to prevent it collapsing.

# Decorating your chocolates

**Chocolate sprinkles**
1 Make a spiral from a 1mm strip, cut it into 50mm (2in) strips and snip off tiny lengths on to a piece of scrap card.

2 Cover the top surface of your chocolate shape in glue and roll it in the sprinkles. Decorate the sides of the chocolate in the same way, once the top has dried.

**Icing strips**
Make a spiral from a 0.5mm paper strip, attach it at one end underneath the chocolate, then wrap it around several times. Glue the spiral underneath when you have finished and snip off the excess.

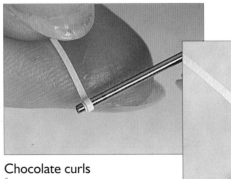

**Chocolate curls**
1 For each curl, coil the end of a 1mm strip three or four times around a quilling tool.

2 Cut off the curl.

# The finished chocolates

Cover a diamond shape in white chocolate sprinkles and glue a 1mm spiral to the top as shown. Make two pegs from 20mm (³⁄₄in), 1mm-wide strips and glue them to the ends.

Cover a dome shape in chocolate sprinkles, make a 1mm spiral and glue it down in a series of loops.

Make a white chocolate dome, then cut 0.5mm strips and glue them across the chocolate. Edge the base with a 1mm-wide strip.

Start with a rectangle and decorate it with a 1mm spiral. Glue it underneath the chocolate at one end and wind round, securing with glue at various intervals.

Cover an oval shape in a square of foil. Fold the excess foil underneath and trim to neaten if necessary.

Cover an oval shape in chocolate sprinkles and decorate it with icing strips (see page 32).

Make a square chocolate and glue a 0.5mm spiral over the top as shown.

Cover a square shape in white chocolate curls, and decorate it with icing strips (see page 32).

Wind and glue a 1mm spiral around a dome-shaped chocolate, starting at the top. Make an 'almond' from a 1mm strip, 112mm (4¹⁄₂in) long, formed into a teardrop.

Make a circle shape using white chocolate-coloured paper. Snip tiny pieces from a 1mm-wide strip, dot glue over the top of the chocolate then sprinkle them on. Glue a 2mm-wide strip around the base.

The final arrangement of chocolates on the lid.

*The finished chocolate box. I have made a selection of different chocolates and scattered these around the base to show you the endless variations that are possible.*

This arrangement of chocolates in a box frame has a fun, contemporary feel. The background of squares was made using a square stencil cut from a piece of card. I drew faint lines on the backing as a guide, then rubbed on two different shades of purple chalk pastel, a square at a time, using crumpled soft tissue paper.

The chocolate gift bag and matching tag shown below would be an appropriate choice for a chocoholic. Just don't forget to put some real chocolates inside the bag!

# Fairies

I have found these fairies so enjoyable to make and I hope you will, too!

No two seem to turn out exactly alike – it is as if they take on characters of their own. This is a design that can be adapted in a number of ways to suit your requirements. Experiment with different hairstyles for instance, or make alternative hats, dresses and shoes. This design includes a wide range of techniques such as looping, spiralling and paper sticks, in addition to conventional quilling.

You will see from the variations that you can use the basic fairy as a starting point and have fun quilling tiny accessories for your fairies to hold.

## You will need

*Head, 2mm strips*
2 pale pink strips, 450mm
(18in) long

Small square of
soft tissue paper

*Body, 3mm strips*
1 dark pink strip, 300mm
(11¾in) long

*Hair, 1mm strips*
2 golden brown strips,
450mm (18in) long

*Dress, 3mm strips*
10 strips in 5 shades of pink (2
strips of each colour), 450mm
(18in) long

1 dark pink strip, 30mm
(1¼in) long, for fringing

*Arms*
2 pieces of pale pink tissue
paper, 25mm (1in) square

*Hands, 2mm strips*
2 pale pink strips, 56mm
(2¼in) long

*Legs*
4 pieces of pale pink tissue
paper, 32mm (1¼in) square

*Feet, 3mm strips*
2 dark pink strips, 112mm
(4½in) long

*Wings, 2mm strips*
3 white strips, 450mm
(18in) long

1 dark pink strip, 450mm
(18in) long

*Tiara, 2mm strips*
1 dark pink strip, 300mm
(11¾in) long

*Other equipment*
Extra fine-pointed felt-tip pens
in black and pink

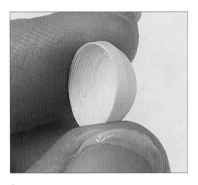

1 For the head, join two pale pink strips together end to end (see page 27), then roll the strip into a solid coil. Dome the coil and squeeze it into an oval shape.

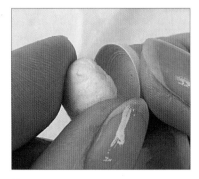

2 Make a tight ball out of soft tissue paper to fit snugly inside the head. Seal it with PVA glue, then glue it inside the fairy's head.

3 Make the body using a teardrop. Pinch out one side to create the waist.

4 Put a dab of glue on the rounded end of the body and push it on to the base of the head. Allow the glue to dry.

5 Now make the fairy's hair. Begin by creating two full-length spirals from the 1mm strips. Start on the top of her head in the centre, apply a strip of glue down the side of the head and attach a length of spiral.

6 Cut the spiral to the required length, then glue on the next section in the same way, gradually working your way around the head. Start each lock of hair from the same point on the top of the fairy's head.

7 Make sure the hair frames the face, without covering too much of it.

8 If your fairy is freestanding, make sure the back of the head is completely covered. (There is no need do this if she is to be mounted on a card or frame.)

9 If necessary, neaten the fairy's hair by trimming it.

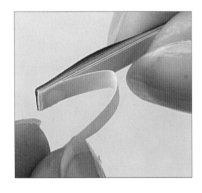

10 Begin the dress. Take the ten 3mm paper strips in five different shades of pink, two strips in each shade. Arrange them in order, from the lightest to the darkest shade. Glue the strips together, one on top of the other, at one end. Make a loop, approximately 10mm (½in) deep, in the first strip (this will form the inner part of the dress). Glue the loop in place at the top.

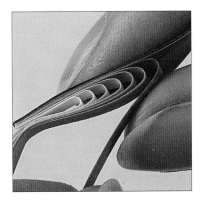

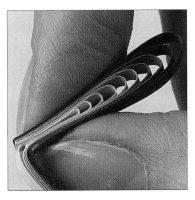

11 Form the remaining strips into loops in the same way, making them progressively longer.

12 When you have made all the loops, bend the strips back on themselves ready to start the next set of loops.

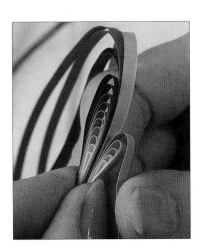

13 Start to form the second set of loops, matching the depth of the loops in the first set as closely as possible.

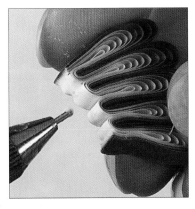

14 Make five sets of loops, and cut off the excess paper to finish.

15 Apply glue to the top of the skirt, ready to attach it to the fairy's body.

16 Push the skirt on to the end of the body and allow the glue to dry.

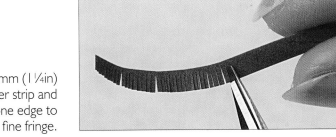

17 Take the 30mm (1 1/4in) length of 3mm paper strip and snip into it along one edge to create a fine fringe.

18 Use this to decorate the top of the fairy's dress. Apply dabs of glue around the top of the dress, lay the fringe over the top and secure it at the back.

19 Place a strip of glue along the inside edges of the two outer loops on either side of the fairy's dress, and push them together to hold the folds in place.

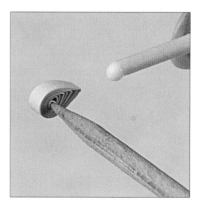

20 For the arms, make two paper sticks from 25mm (1in) square sheets of tissue paper. Make two teardrops for the hands, and glue one to the end of each arm.

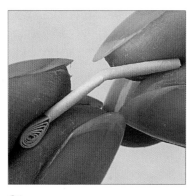

21 Bend each arm in the middle to create an elbow.

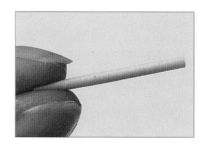

22 Make two more paper sticks for the legs using 32mm (1¼in) squares of tissue paper. Follow the same method as for the arms, though this time use two squares of tissue paper for each limb to make the legs thicker than the arms. Apply a dab of glue to one end of each leg and squash it flat. This makes it easier to attach the legs to the fairy's body.

23 Make two teardrops for the fairy's feet. Place a dab of glue at the tip of each one, and attach the unflattened end of each leg to a foot.

24 Place glue along the edges of the central loop, and insert the legs.

25 Put a dab of glue on the fairy's back and attach both arms. Leave the glue to dry.

26 To begin the wings, take a 2mm white paper strip and put a single loop in the end, approximately 10mm (½in) deep. Secure it with a dab of glue. Bend the paper strip back on itself, ready to form the next loop.

27 Create a total of nine loops for the upper wings, and six for the lower wings. There is no need to glue each loop. Make two upper wings using a full strip for each, and two lower wings using half a strip for each.

28 Push down on the tip of each wing to form it into the correct shape.

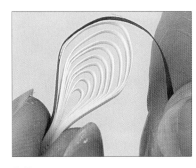

29 Apply glue around the outside of each wing, and attach a pink strip. Wrap it around once, then trim off the excess.

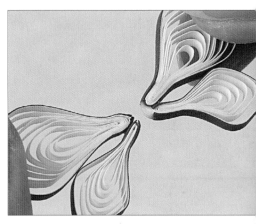

30 Glue each upper wing to a lower wing at their tips, then glue the two pairs of wings together. Allow the glue to dry.

31 Place a dab of glue in the centre of the wings and press the fairy down on them.

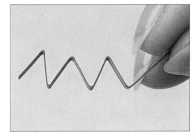

32 For the tiara, make a double-thickness 2mm strip, then when it is dry cut it down to 1mm. Form the strip into a concertina shape with six points. Cut off the excess.

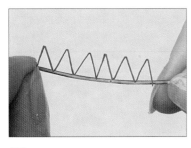 

33 Apply a line of glue to a 40mm (1 ½in) length of the same double-thickness paper strip, even out the points in the concertina shape, and lay it on the strip. Allow the glue to dry thoroughly.

34 Bend the shape round into a circle to form a tiara. Glue the ends together, pushing down on them with the side of a cocktail stick to seal the join. Allow the glue to dry.

35 Put glue around the base of the tiara and attach it to the fairy's head.

36 Using extra fine-pointed felt-tip pens, draw on the fairy's face using two black dots for the eyes and a curved pink line for the mouth.

*The completed fairy.*

The basic fairy design can be easily adapted so that the fairies become angels – these would make a delightful addition to your Christmas tree! Only three loops are used for the dress instead of five, and the number of strips used has been increased to add length. Each wing is made in the same way as the basic fairy wing, but increased in size and pinched into a different shape.

**Opposite**

These green-fingered fairies hold a pot of lavender, a watering can and lavender in a paper trug. To make the trug, glue together 3mm-wide double-thickness strips in a curved shape, then edge the whole thing with another 3mm strip and add a double-thickness strip for the handle. The lavender is made from very thin double-thickness strips covered with glue at one end, and coated with mauve sprinkles, as for the chocolates (see page 32).

The flower pot is made from a tall dome, squashed flat at the base. Glue a loose coil inside then wedge the stems into it before adding some dark brown sprinkles for the soil (see page 32).

The watering can is made from silver-faced paper. Use a 10mm-wide strip for the main part of the can, glued round a large, 3mm-wide peg rolled from a 450mm (18in) long strip. Make a tapered tube for the spout section, finished off with a domed peg. Add handles made from 2mm-wide strips.

These cheerful baking fairies are armed with their own cooking utensils, including a tiny paper whisk! They also wear quilled aprons to protect their fairy clothes. They would make a charming gift for an enthusiastic chef.

The chefs' hats are made from a loose coil rolled from a 5mm-wide strip, 112mm (4½in) long. To make the top section, glue four 25mm (1in) strips in the centre to form a star. Roll each of the eight ends into the centre and remove the tool. Glue the coil into the open centre.

Large pegs have been used to make the jam, plate, saucepan and bowl – the bowl has been domed and then upturned. The 'mixture' inside the bowl is made from tiny curls, as for the chocolates (see page 32). Paper sticks have been used for handles, and the whisk is made from silver spirals formed into loops and gathered at the base. The 'bowl' of the wooden spoon is a small solid coil which has been domed slightly. The jam tarts are made in the same way, with added sprinkles, as for the chocolates (see page 32). The jam jar has been wrapped with clear sticky tape to make it look like glass. The aprons are formed from strips 1mm wide. They are made in two sections, then joined together at the waist with a narrow strip. A small semi-circle has been quilled for the pocket.

# Index

*Detail taken from the box shown on page 29.*